RA
PUI

BUSINESS AND LIFE ....
THE RAJINIKANTH WAY

P.C. Balasubramanian is one of the founder directors of Matrix Business Services India, one of India's leading verification companies. He is passionate about enterprise and institution-building and is of the opinion that it is people who matter the most in any company and loves being able to motivate people in order to bring out the best in them. He believes that one must always give equal importance to one's professional as well as personal life; he is also an ardent admirer of Rajinikanth. It is the coming together of these two elements that provided the motivation for this book.

Raja Krishnamoorthy has over thirty-three years of experience in the field of human resources. He is one of the directors of Talent Maximus India, a Chennai-based HR services organization. As a trainer and consultant in the area of organization development, he does extensive work in team synergy, transformation and leadership skills and personal growth through self-awareness. He is also an actor, explorer and thinks of himself as a student of life.

Visit www.facebook.com/Rajinis.Punchtantra to find out more about the book and the authors.

RAJINI'S
PUNCHTANTRA
BUSINESS AND LIFE MANAGEMENT
THE RAJINIKANTH WAY

P.C. Balasubramanian is one of the founder directors of Matrix Business Services India, one of India's leading verification companies. He is passionate about enterprise and institution-building and is of the opinion that it is people who matter the most in any company and loves being able to provide people in order to bring out the best in them. He believes that one must always give equal importance to one's professional as well as personal life. He is also an avid admirer of Rajinikanth. It is the coming together of these two elements that provides the motivation for this book.

Raja Krishnamoorthy has over thirty years of experience in the field of human resources. He is one of the directors of Talent Maximus India, a Chennai-based HR services organization. As a trainer and consultant in the area of organization development, he does extensive work in team synergy, transformation and leadership skill and personal growth through self-awareness. He is master actor, explorer and takes life as a student of life.

Visit www.facebook.com/RajinisPunchtantra to find out more about the book and the authors.

RAJINI'S
PUNCHTANTRA

BUSINESS AND LIFE MANAGEMENT
THE RAJINIKANTH WAY

P.C. Balasubramanian and **Raja Krishnamoorthy**

RUPA

First published in 2012 by
Rupa Publications India Pvt. Ltd.
7/16, Ansari Road, Daryaganj
New Delhi 110002

Sales Centres:
Allahabad Bengaluru Chennai
Hyderabad Jaipur Kathmandu
Kolkata Mumbai

Photographs courtesy Gnanam,
Film News Anandan and Sundar of onlysuperstar.com

First published in 2010 by New Horizon Media Pvt. Ltd., Chennai,
under the title *Rajini's Punchtantra: Value Statements on Business and Life
Management*. This edition published by arrangement with
the original publisher.

Second impression 2012

ISBN: 978-81-291-1999-5

10 9 8 7 6 5 4 3 2

P.C. Balasubramanian and Raja Krishnamoorthy assert
the moral right to be identified as the authors of this work.

Printed in India by
Rekha Printers Pvt. Ltd.
A-102/1, Okhla Industrial Area, Phase II
New Delhi 110020

Dedicated to Rajinikanth
and all his fans and admirers

Contents

Foreword

Tamil cinema has been a fountainhead of political ideologies and revolutionary thoughts. That it has managed to seamlessly weave social purpose with popular entertainment is its uniqueness.

Rajinikanth is a phenomenon nonpareil in Tamil cinema. He is fascinating as much for his striking 'style' movements as for his deeply insightful punchlines. His strength lies in effortlessly combining mass appeal with sincerity of purpose. Rajinikanth's off-screen life and conduct have vastly added credibility to his on-screen image and character. It is no wonder that Rajini is eponymous with his punchlines, which are laden with meaning.

The authors, P.C. Balasubramanian and Raja Krishnamoorthy, should be warmly complimented for collecting together Rajini's pearls of wisdom and showcasing their brilliance. The authors are not uninformed fans given to irrational idolatry. One is a successful entrepreneur and the other a well-respected consultant. That both have found Rajini's signature statements deeply relevant to management practices and, indeed, life at large is testimony to the true value of Rajini's punchlines. It is also telling proof of Rajini's appeal among people in all walks of life.

The annotations provided in this book are lucid and friendly, yet deep and thoughtful—just like a Rajinikanth movie!

R. Seshasayee
Executive Vice Chairman, Ashok Leyland

Introduction

Once in a while, in history, there appears someone whose message provides hope, lights a spark and energizes all of mankind. It is never quite the message itself but who said it, how and when, that makes it significant. Often these messages are simple and earthy; yet, coming from this personality, they grow alive and powerful. They acquire significance, wide acceptance and are etched in public memory. So it is with Rajinikanth. His punchlines have had such a deep impact on me that it became my mission to make a book out of them.

I have grown up watching Rajinikanth films—nothing new in that, most of my generation did. But, unlike many adolescent obsessions that you grow out of as you mature, I have not been able to grow out of my fascination with his punchlines. As I grew older—and, hopefully, wiser—I soaked in deeper their meaning. The impact they made on me and a whole lot of others is remarkable.

From a coolie to a CEO, from a small-time entrepreneur to a big businessman, from an urchin to a postgraduate, from a maid to an activist, from lovers to siblings, from spouses to in-laws—I have seen 'Rajini dialogues' evoke deep resonance in all, often accompanied by a sparkle in the eye, a nod of acceptance and a smile of acknowledgement. The statements have touched them and remained deep within.

I call these 'value statements', for only such statements travel a long distance, remain in the minds and hearts of people for generations and are quoted in their conversations. I have encountered people from different walks of life who quote Rajini's punchlines at work or home or social gatherings in order to communicate their views in a simple but powerful manner. And, most of the time, the lines are found relevant, enjoyed and accepted well. This is why it has perhaps become a Rajinikanth tradition that millions of his fans (and many others who might have not seen the particular film in question) look forward to these value statements from the superstar—not just in his movies but also at public forums where he may be delivering a speech.

Hence I recognize that, in their mass appeal, their potential to entertain, their power to educate and awaken society and make an impression on the minds of millions, these value statements are waiting to be leveraged for wider impact. That, essentially, is the purpose of this book.

In a way, Rajini's own life is his message. It has been a journey of hardship, struggle, dreams, superstardom, learning, responsibility, resisting temptation, simplicity, utmost humility—and being a role model for generations of people. And, in the process, Rajini has woven such magic in the minds of millions that his mere utterances have turned into gems of wisdom.

I salute this living legend, with reverence and admiration. This book is an effort to chronicle a part of his contribution to society and document it for posterity—so that future generations too can enjoy, cherish and learn from them.

P.C. Balasubramanian

Chennai

'I am amazed to see the creativity, interpretation and the strong relevance of some of the punchlines in both business and life management. I appreciate the good work of P.C. Balasubramanian, who has penned this interesting book along with Raja Krishnamoorthy. I hope that all readers, including my fans, would enjoy reading this book.'

~Value Statement~

Film: *Padaiyappa*

'En vazhi thanee vazhi'

'MY WAY IS
A UNIQUE WAY'

In Business

This applies to good organizations which have a unique work culture, exclusive products or services, and those that build their reputation through differentiated value creation for various stakeholders. The unique selling proposition (USP) of an organization needs to go beyond its product or service. Genuine care for its customers and other stakeholders, unique value creation for its investors and creating a sense of ownership as well as inspiring a sense of pride and belonging in its employees—the *thanee vazhi* for a corporation can indeed be very special.

You need to be different to succeed. Don't choose a 'me too' line of business or a 'me too' way of running a company. Even if you do, you need to look at some differentiators, without which your growth may not be fast or sustained.

A close look at this mantra tells us clearly that we need to avoid a herd mentality even in business. Recent history talks of many failures on account of herd mentality—the failure of many dot-coms is a case in point. Some of the differentiators could be the marketing strategies, technology in use, packaging, distribution and sales, and even the targeted market. Today, it is the differentiator that can give one the opportunity to be noticed and grow faster.

In Life

This statement underlines the importance of every person's ability to showcase his or her uniqueness. Most human beings, by definition, traverse the pathway of paradoxical living. On the one hand, people are caught up in the conventional way of life, looking for common trends, seeking what is fashionable, keeping up with the Joneses; and yet, at a deeper level, each one wants to be respected for what is different about him or her and would want to have his or her own unique identity.

This value statement also clearly communicates the importance of leading one's own life. Never become prey to herd mentality. Only when one thinks differently would many options be available. But this statement should not be misinterpreted: while it motivates and encourages you to think independently, it doesn't imply that you need to always disagree with the majority just to prove a point.

Message
Differentiate yourself; have a distinct identity

~*Value Statement* ~

Film: *Basha*

'Naan oru thadavai sonna, nooru thadava sonna maadhiri'

★

'If I say something once, it is equivalent to saying it a hundred times'

In Business

Communication is not just about what you say but also how you say it. It is, in a way, an irreversible act: no one gets a second chance to make a first impression. This statement takes communication to the next level—beyond the concept that it is best achieved by a congruence of words, tone of voice and facial expressions. It promulgates two cardinal rules: achieve clarity ('use your head') but give unswerving commitment ('give your heart') to stand by what has been stated. To accomplish this, the communicator needs foresight, sensitivity to the context of the recipient, a deep understanding of the effect of one's words on the listener and the ability to use clear language to drive home the point. And once you have made your point, you need to let the other person absorb it at his or her own pace. Effective communication does not necessarily occur just because something is repeated a hundred times.

The statement also highlights the responsibility of the listener. The listener must pay undivided attention to the words and intent of the communicator, leading to total absorption of the message. Thus, for the listener, the statement should be modified as *oru thadavai ketta, nooru thadava ketta maathiri*— 'what is heard once is to be treated as if heard a hundred times'.

In Life

Communication is also sharing. In order to have meaningful relationships in life and society, one must be able to share one's thoughts with one's friends, family and in all social interactions. According to writer and management consultant Peter F. Drucker, 'The most important thing in communication is hearing what isn't said.' This too we must keep in mind. We have to not only understand what is being said to us, and in exchange convey to the listener what we want to say, but also learn to interpret what remains unsaid in a particular situation. This statement can thus be interpreted as an emphasis on understanding the nuances of conversation and thus communicating effectively with everyone. Effective and proper communication builds better relationships and helps in retaining important ones.

Message
Communicate effectively

Film: *Sivaji*

'Paera kaetavudane chumma athuruthilae'

'The mere mention of [his] name causes tremors'

In Business

In the corporate world, reputation is the result of innovation (for example: Google), integrity and trust (for example: the Tata group), creativity (for example: Disney) and product innovation (for example: Apple). It calls for unparalleled mastery in the chosen area or unblemished reputation and standing through decades of existence.

This powerful value statement underscores the importance of the creation of 'brands' and safeguarding brand equity. It also highlights the importance of building and sustaining one's reputation. Both of these can be achieved in the long run with sustained effort. Reputation-building adds great value to the organization in the eyes of the customers, staff, investors, regulatory authorities and society at large. Once this reputation has been built, it is even more important to maintain and enhance it through consistent performance and delivery.

A brand communicates trust and acceptance and, in most cases, it takes years to create one. A lot of care must be taken to ensure that the mere mention of the brand name would make the desired impact in the market.

In Life

All human beings are keen to have their own individual and well-respected identity. It is this identity that distinguishes one from the rest of the crowd. Such an identity could be construed as the style/personality/image of the person that sets him or her apart. When there is quality, strength and value for all to see, there is great respect and admiration for the person. With reference to such people, it is common to say: *avar pera sonnalae pothum*—just mentioning his or her name creates a phenomenal impact; and here we are talking about *paera kettale athiruthulae*—the mere mention of the name leads to tremors and vibrations. It is necessary, however, that this impact is felt because of the positive qualities of the person and not on account of fear, anxiety or insecurity caused by the individual.

Message
Build an impeccable reputation

Film: *Annamalai*

**'Naan solrathaiyum seiven...
sollaathathaiyum seiven'**

'I will deliver
what I promise...
and deliver even
what I didn't'

In Business

The foundation of lasting self-confidence and self-esteem is excellence—mastery of your work. This value statement takes the management mantra of excellence and simplifies it: beat expectations in whatever is to be done.

According to Buck Rodgers, the legendary American baseball player, manager and coach, 'There are countless ways of attaining greatness, but any road to reaching one's maximum potential must be built on a bedrock of respect for the individual, a commitment to work excellence and a rejection of mediocrity.' *Sollaathathaiyum seiven*—delivering what is promised—emphasizes this required trait for a list which can be endless: upping sales, adding clients, cutting down wastage, improving productivity, boosting the morale of human resources, better asset utilization, and so on.

The entire value statement is very true for customer services—as the famous businessman and entrepreneur Sam Walton had said, 'The goal as a company is to have customer service that is not just the best but legendary.' It also reminds one that for sustaining growth the search for excellence should remain consistent and constant.

In Life

The true success of a person's life is directly proportional to his commitment to achieve, exceed expectations and scale excellence, regardless of his or her chosen field. A positive attitude and constant self-motivation are two important traits that will enable anyone to accomplish more than expected—*sollaathathu*.

Excellence can be achieved if you care more than what others think wise, risk more than what others think safe, dream higher than what others think practical, expect more than what others think possible. This principle can be taken even further if one is able to adopt and implement in one's life the Greek philosopher Aristotle's statement: 'Excellence is an art won by training and habituation. We do not act rightly because we have virtue or excellence, but we rather have those because we have acted rightly. We are what we repeatedly do. Excellence, then, is not an act but a habit.'

Message
Surprise others, go beyond expectations

~Value Statement~

5

Film: *Baba*

**'Naan yosikkaama pesa maataen,
pesina piragu yosikka maataen'**

★

**'I think before I speak, and
don't doubt what I say'**

In Business

What are the qualities of a good communicator? Clarity of thought, foresight, deep contemplation and analysis of the subject matter, consideration of the possible impact of the communication, delivery of the idea and a readiness to deal with the impact of the communication. Such is the quality that defines good leaders and policymakers. They have enormous responsibilities to and for a large population and their decisions have a lasting impact. Once such a considered decision has been taken, there is no wavering of mind about its sanctity.

A mature leader understands that taking a considered decision does not mean that it will not encounter any hurdles in implementation. These are recognized by him or her as they arise. Active collaboration from team members is sought and issues are dealt with. There is also a mentoring and grooming role played by the leader to help his or her team face up to the challenges of implementation and not be paralysed by helplessness. He or she simply stands by the dictum that you cannot become intelligent in retrospect.

Such an approach ensures that all the required homework and analysis is done prior to any major decision. Once the decision is taken and clearly communicated to the team, the entire team needs to be highly focused on the attainment of the objective. This value statement also communicates the duty of the management to back the team even when things don't fall into place as per expectations in the short run.

In Life

Every human being goes through these phases of decision-making in life, be it a choice of education, life partner, friends or material possessions or investments. The sources of conflict in these situations are inherent self-doubt, lack of confidence and inadequate guidance and mentoring from family systems. This value statement teaches us the simple philosophy of staying committed to what we say or do. At the same time, it also cautions us to think about what we say before we do so, how we say it, what we promise or commit to and how we pass judgement. Once you commit to something, even a relationship, you need to cross the hurdles you may face from time to time, unless you want to choose the most convenient—and undesirable—option of breaking your commitment.

Message
Carefully deliberate on what you wish to commit to, but do not hesitate once you have committed

Film: *Muthu*

'Naan eppo varuven eppadi varuvennu yarukkum theriyathu...aana varavendiya nerathile correctaa varuven'

★

'No one knows when and how I will come...but I will be there at the right time'

In Business

This statement underlines the importance of timeliness and the ability to surprise pleasantly. Ralph Waldo Emerson says in *The Conduct of Life*, '[T]he art of getting rich consists not in industry, much less in saving, but in a better order, in timeliness, in being at the right spot.' One might call it the 'Hanuman' effect. This timeliness is the characteristic of a person who is an embodiment of immense capability, agility and reliability. Others in the system would depend heavily on such a person to deliver the goods. They may even have extraordinary expectations from him or her—he or she may be expected to act as a saviour in different situations.

So who performs such a rescue act? That individual—or even organization—who is 'different' and larger than life, someone who almost comes out of nowhere at the right time and surprises the dependent parties with a necessary solution—like Hanuman arriving with the Sanjeevani at the right time.

Many organizations in the last twenty years have acted as corporate Hanumans—Google, for search engines; Amazon, for publishing; Facebook, for social networking; Maruti 800, for small passenger cars; and Nokia, for handsets—exemplifying the value statement we are discussing here. In addition, it is important to remember that most Japanese businesses are centred on their traditional proverb: 'You win battles by knowing about the enemy's timing, and using a timing which the enemy does not expect.'

In Life

Life is all about timing. The unreachable becomes reachable, the unavailable becomes available and the unattainable attainable—if the timing is right. In any given situation, have patience, wait it out. It is all about timing. One of the first lessons we learn in our lives is to be punctual. How often have we missed a train, bus or flight because of delays at our end? Rarely. This is because when we are late, a train or an aircraft does not wait for us. But we don't give the same importance to punctuality in most of the other areas of life, thus making others lose confidence in us. It is extremely undesirable to make others wait for us: we need to value their time. This quality has to be practised to perfection.

The lesson this value statement teaches us is that we need to be present where our presence is required in order to create the right impact. If our duty demands our presence, we need to make it—irrespective of how we manage to get there. This is part of our social obligation. Our sense of timing and commitment defines how dependable we are.

Message
Create the right impact at the right time

Film: *Yejaman*

'Neenga sattapadi dharmam pannanumunu solreenga, naan dharmam panratha sattama vechukiren'

★

'You say that one must do good as stated by law, whereas I believe that doing good is the law'

In Business

Business and philanthropy, in general, don't come together. For those organizations that do make an effort to contribute to a social cause, insincerity and hypocrisy are not uncommon—at best, it is an attempt at getting tax exemptions; at worst, it is a publicity gimmick. It is widely believed that the purpose of a business is to maximize returns to its shareholders, and it is responsible only to its shareholders and not to society as a whole. Despite this notion, businesses worldwide have indulged in charity.

As Albert Einstein said, 'It is every man's obligation to put back into the world at least the equivalent of what he takes out of it.' Many shareholders who have benefited from the profits of their business have also done the same—for instance, the Bill and Melinda Gates Foundation, the Infosys Foundation, the Buffet Foundation and the Tata trusts.

Corporate social responsibility (CSR) is the new evolving mantra of the corporate world. But CSR is not regulatory, so it is up to companies to devise their own policies to become philanthropic or socially responsible. This is exactly what the value statement embodies—only when corporate bodies devise their policy agenda from within, obtain stakeholders' approval and take it up as a cause, along with their profit goals, will they transform their identity from a reputable business to a good corporate citizen.

In Life

The poet Kannadasan reaffirms this principle through the famous line 'Charity will save your name' in the title song from the film *Dharmam Thalai Kaakkum*. In that song, he says 'Charity will also save your life at the right time, what you give will stand in good stead all your life.' At its best, 'Charity will make your worst enemy stand in shame at your doorstep.' That is the power of charity.

'No person is ever honoured for what he received. Honour has been the reward for what he gave,' Calvin Coolidge had said. This value statement boldly asks you to make it your personal law to contribute your efforts to a social cause. It is the effort that counts—your contribution need not be monetary. The statement gives us the message that if every one of us apportions a small share of our efforts towards a charitable objective, the world will become a better place to live in.

Message
Give back to society at least a portion what you gain from it—make this mandatory within yourself

~Value Statement~

8

Film: *Dharmathin Thalaivan*

*'Nan thatti kaetpaen, aana,
kotti kudupaen'*

*

'I question hard
(the wrongdoer)
and reward generously
(the deserving)'

In Business

Management theorists have called this the 'carrot and stick' approach for team leaders: incentive through reward and deterrence by punishment. The end objective is to bring about a change in the behaviour of team members by using either. This value statement also goes beyond the 'carrot and stick' approach in the sense that it advocates that the carrot be ultimately given to the performer.

Thatti kaetpaen is the stick in action—pulling up the errant team member, demanding attention to what is essential and thus needs more focus, censuring when the behaviour of a team member affects the performance of the team. The stick—or fear—is a good motivator, and when used at the appropriate time, can produce the desired change. When all other influencers fail, the stick approach is the most effective as it produces fear, leading to instant compliance and immediate results.

Kotti kudupaen is the carrot, or motivation through reward. Most managers easily take on the *kotti kudupaen* approach, without much heed to *thatti kaetpaen*. In organizations, this approach reaches a crescendo in the annual performance appraisal process. It is widely seen that managers, without delving much into performance factors, tend to recommend even below-average employees for incentives, rewards and goodies—sometimes to boost their own popularity among employees. The result of this misuse of the carrot approach is often a deluge of undeserving recommendations, creating pressure for undeserved rewards, thereby leading to disproportionate reward systems. Consequently, truly deserving candidates are overlooked while undeserving ones are glorified.

A true leader manages both the carrot and the stick very well. He or she separates the wheat from the chaff and follows a simple, disciplined approach to performance—enabling and ensuring the right behaviour, whilst preventing and prohibiting the wrong one.

In Life

We generally tend to treat reward and punishment as mutually exclusive. In today's world, parents seem to be too indulgent with their children, but they largely 'outsource' the responsibility to discipline to external units such as schools, teachers or other authorities. Similar situations of manipulation can be seen in a larger social context as well. Society suffers when populist governments mindlessly give away freebies and facilities without due deference to eligibility and accountability. We are living at a time when there is total absence of any demand by leaders for accountability from followers; at the same time, there is in evidence a deep desire to appear charitable and benevolent by pampering the public.

Imbibing the lesson *thatti kaetpaen, aana, kotti kudupaen* will hugely benefit the political leaders of today, as well as every single human being, so that they may build a lasting and devoted support base for all life situations.

Message
Instil discipline through judicious reward and punishment

Film: *Baba*

'Khatham...khatham...mudinjathu mudinju potchu'

✳

'Let bygones be bygones'

In Business

There is a popular saying: 'One reason God created time was so that there would be a place to bury the failures of the past.' That philosophy is exactly what this statement embodies. If history were all there is to the business game, then the richest corporations would be mere libraries. In many organizations, a lot of productive time is wasted in digging through past data and reviewing instances of project failure, unsuccessful growth or overspent budgets. While review is important and critical, there is no need to spend too much time and energy in pondering on the past beyond what is required for learning and correction.

In many review meetings, this entrenchment with the past predominates and the big picture—looking at the future— is forgotten. Reviewing should be a process which aims at transforming acquired information into empowerment through action—otherwise it boils down to regression and fault-finding. One must learn from the past, watch the present and create the future. Change is the only constant in life, and those who look only to the past or present are certain to miss future opportunities for progress and improvement.

In Life

Life coach Anthony Robbins says, 'It's not what's happening to you now or what has happened in your past that determines who you become. Rather, it's your decision about what to focus on, what things mean to you, and what you are going to do about them that will determine your ultimate destiny.' How true!

Life is all about moving on. This value statement stresses the importance of looking ahead. It can be further extended to mean that we should forget, forgive and celebrate life. What we need to remember about the past is that it has all worked together to bring us to this very moment, and we can now seize the opportunity to start anew and make everything right. It gently reminds us to deal with one day at a time: don't look back, take care of the present and make it worth remembering...the future will take care of you.

Message
Bury the past and look forward

10

Film: *Engeyo Kaeta Kural*

*'Kai alavu kaasu iruntha athu
nambala kaappathum, athuve
kazhuthu varai iruntha atha
namma kappathunum'*

★

'If you have a handful of
money, it will take care of you;
if you have too much wealth,
you will have to take
care of it'

In Business

This upholds the dharmic principle encapsulated in the words of Jeffrey Bryant: 'Diligent accumulation of personal wealth is not inherently ungodly so long as it is complemented by equally diligent distribution of personal wealth.' *Kai alavu kaasu* literally means a handful of money or the limited wealth necessary for survival and maintenance. One should aim at accumulation of sufficient resources for one's economic well-being and peace of mind. *Kazhuthu alavu kaasu*, or being neck deep in riches, leads to entrapment in the desire to amass wealth out of personal greed—thus depriving the business of productive investments, the shareholders of their legitimate returns and other stakeholders of their dues.

This statement underlines the importance of fair distribution of income and inclusive growth. Businesses are not cisterns for hoarding; rather, they are channels for sharing. Progressive organizations are lean and hungry because they believe in inclusive growth, where all the stakeholders—shareholders, employees and the government—are given their fair share of the company's surplus. As a part of its corporate responsibility, every organization should be proud to exhibit this distribution-of-surplus mentality.

In Life

Kazhuthu alavu kaasu—being neck deep in riches—represents the greedy, self-indulgent accumulator of wealth. As quickly as one amasses wealth, so is one trapped by anxiety about how much wealth has been amassed and insecurities over the possibility of losing it. Often one begins to suspect the people around and doubt their motives, to the extent of losing one's peace of mind over the protection of this wealth. Mahatma Gandhi aptly said that there is enough food in the world for every hungry man's need but not enough for even one man's greed. Money-making should not lead to mindless money-chasing.

Message
Practise inclusive growth and the fair distribution of surplus

Film: *Basha*

'Pon, penn, pugazh pinnadi ambalai poga koodathu, ambalainga pinnala ithellam varanum'

✶

'Don't chase wealth, women and fame; these should follow you'

In Business

In today's corporate culture, you may wonder as to whether this is a moralistic statement. Far from it. This statement highlights the importance of staying focused on your target. Be clear about what has to be delivered, remain focused on the process that will take you there, and keep at it. This is the pathway of the karma yogi—we also call this the 'charisma' effect.

Natural leaders pull these factors—wealth, fame and adulation—towards themselves effortlessly, with dignity and grace. They realize that there is a greater agenda waiting to be addressed, are completely focused on the task and are passionately working towards a better purpose or creating a better world. Their dedication is unparalleled, not contaminated by trivial personal needs and other fatal temptations. Greatness is naturally bestowed on such people. Across nations, we have stories of people with humble beginnings rising to great statures as a result of sheer dedication. From Abraham Lincoln to Dr A.P.J. Abdul Kalam, there are several shining examples to prove this.

If our aspiration is supported by good work, dedication, quality output and increased productivity, thereby benefiting the organization, rewards will automatically follow. It is all about staying focused and channelling one's entire energy and resources towards the objective. Aspirations are vital, but they alone don't fetch the organization the desired results. This logic holds good for any manager.

In Life

A deeper analysis of this statement brings out the importance of maintaining one's self-respect and dignity. Simply put: don't chase money and wealth, earn it; don't waste precious time—especially your youth—save it; don't chase a seat or a position just to gain power. If you want to live with dignity, earn through proper means and methods instead of just yearning for what you desire. Stay focused and be diligent—rewards will follow automatically.

Message
Earn, don't yearn; don't strive desperately for glory—wait for your rewards

~*Value Statement*~

Film: *Arunachalam*

★

'Sollraan, seiaraan'

'He (the higher one) instructs, I do'

In Business

Sollraan (the boss—the higher power) instructs, *seiaraan* (the subordinate—the follower or team member) executes. The value statement spells out the first golden rule of management: delegate, don't try to do everything by yourself because you simply can't. General George S. Patton had once said, 'Never tell people how to do things. Tell them what to do, and they will surprise you with their ingenuity.' At one level, delegation is about setting broad guidelines by the one who delegates; whilst at another level, the delegated converts the guidelines to actionable instructions through unswerving adherence. Delegation places a complex responsibility on the policymaker—he or she can delegate authority but never his or her responsibility.

On the doer's part, it is the ability to recognize the value of good policies, the commitment as a good soldier and the consistent avoidance of improper shortcuts and circumvention that can lead to excellence. Good business practices always centre on policies and standard operating procedures (SOPs), service-level agreements vouching for an organization's reliability, repeatability and predictability of products and services. SOPs in business simply represent the instructions—*sollraan*.

In Life

One of the fundamental tenets of Indian family culture—respecting one's elders—is based on this principle. From ancient times, joint family structures have recognized the need for systematic decision-making and information flow. This necessitated a clear role for policymakers and implementers, leading to easy conversion of instructions into action and clarity of job roles. It required reverence for the decision-makers (elders) and ego-free acceptance on part of the implementers (youngsters).

Indian mythology has many illustrations of this principle, best exemplified by the way instructions were followed by Lord Rama. Japanese and Chinese family cultures too are renowned for the practice of this principle. As a nation and state, Singapore exemplifies how a democratic state can achieve excellence with strict adherence to the policies laid down by the state—an amazing evidence of great policymaking and even greater execution. Simply put, in Singapore, the state is *sollraan* and the citizens are *seiaraan*. One can easily think of other instances in society where this principle is practised.

Message
Judicious delegation and proper implementation produce the desired results

~Value Statement~

13

Film: *Johnny*

*'Intha ulagathule ethu aeduthalum,
onnaiveda onnu betteragathan therium'*

✳

**'In this world, in any situation,
one option will always look
better than the other'**

In Business

Quality is often misconstrued as that which is the best, but in simple terms it means fitness for purpose. Without this maturity of perspective, we keep getting distracted by something that appears 'even better'. How does one escape this quagmire of comparison and make up one's mind?

Often, in the anxious pursuit of ultimate quality—where one product or service appears better than the other, constantly—the 'here-and-now opportunity' perspective is lost. Peter Drucker warns businesses when he says, 'Quality in a product or service is not what the supplier puts in. It is what the customer gets out and is willing to pay for. A product is not quality because it is hard to make or costs a lot of money, as manufacturers typically believe. This is incompetence. Customers pay only for what is of use to them and gives them value. Nothing else constitutes quality.'

Often in the corporate world, whether it pertains to people, products, services or vendors, delays occur in the pursuit of the 'best'. In this quest for quality, corporates need to remind themselves of what William A. Foster has said: 'Quality is never an accident; it is always the result of high intention, sincere effort, intelligent direction and skilful execution. It represents the wise choice of alternatives.' In fact, what seems to be good today may not always remain good in the ever-changing world of business. Is there anything called the best? One must be sure that the 'best' does not become the evil of the current good.

In Life

It does not take much strength to do things, but it requires great strength to decide what to do. This value statement reminds us that we are always faced with the mirage of the 'best', resulting in a continual search for a better option—the dilemma of whether we are consciously making a right choice and the reality of our committing to something particular at the present moment.

In our personal lives too, we are often unsure if we have made the right decisions. And many often experience disappointments arising out of comparisons and peer pressure. The lesson for us is that we need to make peace with our choices and carry on happily with our lives. Too many comparisons only add pressure and make one feel dissatisfied. We must embrace the words of Theodore Roosevelt: 'In any moment of decision, the best thing you can do is the right thing, the next best is the wrong thing and the worst thing you can do is nothing'; we must make a choice and act accordingly, without being paralysed by the thought that there might be a better course of action available to us.

Message
The grass is always greener on the other side

~Value Statement~

Film: *Manithan*

**'Sollarathaithan seivaen...
seiyarathathan solvaen'**

✱

'I do what I say...I say only what I do'

In Business

In his book, *Corporate Truth: The Limits to Transparency*, author Adrian Henriques states, 'Corporate transparency is crucial because, with all their power, companies have a mind of their own. It means that unless people within companies can be honest with themselves, real transparency may be unattainable.'

The root of all corporate scandals is the lack of transparency. Integrity is the lifeline of all individual, corporate and social wellness. Honesty, truth, transparency and genuineness are some of the characteristics that help foster this quality. How relevant is this in today's corporate world, where the focus is completely on seeking opportunity, profitability, capability, investments, market capitalization, technology and competency, with the inevitable erosion of values, principles, integrity and transparency! A cursory glance at the examples of Enron, Lehman Brothers and our own Satyam stands testimony to this erosion.

Speaking the truth is the easiest and most comfortable way of existence, and also the most beneficial. So how do larger social systems—corporates, government and state—show and nurture transparency? By following the Gandhian principle of *satyameva jayate* (the truth prevails). This personal measure of integrity is far more important than over-hyped statements of corporate governance. Do the published corporate documents, advertisement claims, warranties and guarantees stand the test of truth? Ask yourself, and you will know the answer. Truth alone wins in the long run.

In Life

Honesty has a beautiful and refreshing simplicity about it. No ulterior motives. No hidden meanings. Absence of hypocrisy, duplicity, political games and verbal superficiality. It is very difficult to always speak the truth, yet the fact remains that the truth finally brings triumph despite the hardships we may face along the way. Absence of truth can get in the way of any relationship. The only way to develop and maintain a relationship is by being true to each other.

'A man is never more truthful than when he acknowledges himself as a liar,' said the author Mark Twain. 'When in doubt, tell the truth.' He further said, 'Always tell the truth. That way you don't have to remember what you said.' This is something well worth remembering.

It is also important for us to create an environment for others in which they feel encouraged to tell the truth without fear and hesitation. As Martin Luther had said, 'Peace if possible, truth at all costs.'

Message
In the end, the truth always triumphs

15

Film: *Basha*

'Nallavangala aandavan sodhippaan,
kaivida maatan... Kettavangaluku
aandavan neraya kuduppan,
aana kai vittuviduvan'

✴

**'God tests good people but
does not let them down...
He may give the bad ones
generously but lets
them down'**

In Business

There is a popular saying: 'When the going gets tough, the tough get going.' Who are these toughs we are referring to? These are solid and principled organizations—sensitive, proactive, tolerant and with sharing-the-surplus mentality—which conduct themselves with positive intent and action. *Nallavan*, the good organization, is the epitome of these virtues.

These organizations are not short-term oriented, they do not manipulate people and situations and they are not opportunists eyeing a quick gain. They are aware that they have many a mountain to climb and quite a few deserts to traverse. Have we not come across organizations put to severe tests because of political motives? The stronger and principled ones don't give up and emerge stronger out of adversity as their intentions are noble. Ultimately, success and joy are rightfully theirs—such is the saga of the *nallavan*. Even a change in any policy, process, technology or marketing methods may initially lead to a lot of challenges and/or resistance before they produce the desired results. Sustenance, tolerance and patience are very vital factors to cross all hurdles unscathed and finally emerge victorious.

On the other hand, the manipulative opportunists—the *kettavan,* or the bad organizations—seem to gain in the short run, but such gain is only an illusion. Life has a way of playing tricks and short-term gains fade away as quickly as they come, and then the free fall to nowhere happens. Many a time, we have seen organizations vanish into oblivion after some initial gains made through misrepresentation of facts and even resorting to other fraudulent practices.

In Life

This value statement clearly brings out the truth that good human beings—*nallavan*—when tested by God, are aware of the hardships they need to face, and by being tolerant, proactive and humble, they emerge winners in the long run and lead a peaceful life. On the other hand, a bad human being —*kettavan*—who gains by resorting to unlawful and dishonest means, despite being given time by God to recover from this path fails to change, ultimately loses everything—right from wealth, health and good friends to acceptance by society at large.

Message
Don't be swayed by transient challenges and illusory triumphs

~*Value Statement*~

Film: *Arunachalam*

'Paathu vaelai seiyunga…paarkum pothu vellai seiyatheenga'

★

'Be focused and watchful while working, but don't work just because you are being watched'

In Business

This statement asks the proverbial question: are you responsible enough to be self-managed or do you need to be supervised all the time? The statement highlights the difference between the 'achiever' and the 'also-ran'. The achiever is self-motivated, self-disciplined and self-reviewing, thus being self-managed.

The emerging concept of self-directed teams in corporate organizations is an idea derived out of such responsible role-holders. These people do not require constant supervision, control and correction. Their sense of ownership is very high and they treat the resources of the organization as their own. There is a very high value placed on timely and qualitative delivery, and a great sense of personal disappointment and guilt in case of failure, which is readily acknowledged by them.

On the other hand, there is also a large population of employees who need constant 'watching'. Organizations waste considerable managerial time and effort in the unproductive exercise of keeping a tab on employees' performance. The tendency of such employees is to provide only 'evidence' of performance under such watchful situations. When not under watch, they slide into a state of indifference and irresponsibility. Such employees are nothing but added burden for their organizations.

In Life

How relevant is this statement to the Indian philosophy of conscious living? It implies that, at all points of time, there is a need for being aware: of yourself, your context, your environment and your responsibilities in any situation. Highly valuable for both one's personal and professional life, this value statement is even more applicable to when it comes to family. One must bear the responsibilities towards one's family because one recognizes the need to do so rather than out of a concern for what people might say about one. For instance, taking care of one's children's education and future, securing one's financial freedom especially for old age, healthcare, handling the needs of one's parents in their old age, responsibilities towards one's neighbourhood, etc.: one should do this not because society is watching but out of love and the awareness of one's eternal debts and duties. This principle reinforces the simple philosophy of *aham brahmasmi*—self-governance.

Message
Be self-driven and not supervision-driven

Film: *Sivaji*

'*Panningathaan kootama varum, singam singlathan varum*'

'Swine travel in droves, but the lion comes alone'

In Business

An organization that is the foremost in its field and stands apart for its excellence and success is one that forges ahead like the roaring lion rather than like a swine which is governed by what others like itself are doing. This value statement urges organizations to have the courage and confidence of a lion in order to succeed and progress. Their actions must have the same impact as the roar of a lion. This statement can be interpreted as a directive to take adversity head on. One cannot cower and hide in a crowd when a predator is on the prowl—one must be the predator. This value statement should be used to recall the qualities of a lion.

One must be brave like the lion. Being brave is not about foolhardy acts and bravado; it is about withstanding misfortune, hardship, difficulty and danger. Business is about searching for opportunities and treading towards them with a brave front. One must fight when necessary. Lions don't pick fights, but they don't give an inch when their territory or their peace is in danger; a good business organization fights only when its values are challenged. Business managers fight unnecessarily over 'territory' in the guise of protecting but, in reality, give up on their colleagues, ethics and beliefs for safeguarding their position and personal stake. This value statement will remind them to fight only when necessary.

Lions hunt only for essentials—they hunt only when they are hungry, and no more. And they know the what, when and how of hunting. They don't pursue anything that is unnecessary or is beyond their capability. Business and individuals thus have much to learn from the lion, especially on their journey to reach the top without compromising their values, ethics and conduct. A group of lions is known as a pride. There is no better example than the pride of a lion that a business leader can learn from when it comes to safeguarding and appreciation of the team. It is as important to take care of the well-being of your team, your colleagues and business partners who team up with you and enable you succeed as it is to take pride in their accomplishments and protect them from all outside harm.

In Life

The example of the lion also teaches us that we must see ourselves as part of a proud community—whether it is family, a group of friends or the whole nation. One must always aspire to be a lion throughout one's life—the strict adherence to one's principles and ethics, the protection of one's fellows and dependants, the courage to face all adversities and challenges, the instinct to not only survive but be the winner in any competition.

Life is about overcoming roadblocks and marching forward to eternal happiness. If one tries to live according to the teachings of the fearless lion, one can find contentment and lead a life that is joyous and filled with the love and respect of one's associates.

Message
Live like a lion—be brave, protect others, lead the way for everyone

~Value Statement~

18

Film: *Baba*

*'Asanthaa adikarathu unga policy,
asaraama adikarathu Baba policy'*

✳

'Hitting out when the other's
guard is down is your policy,
being ever-vigilant is
Baba's policy'

In Business

There is nothing healthier than an organization's ability to elevate itself through conscious efforts rather than unscrupulous means. The truly successful organization is proactive and principled, succeeding on its own strengths instead of cashing in on the weakness or limitations of its competitors. Business Is not about winning or losing, it's about how fairly you play the game.

You bat straight when you are proactive. One of the successful habits advocated by Stephen Covey, the author of *The Seven Habits of Highly Effective People,* is being principle-centred and proactive: 'If you are proactive, you don't have to wait for circumstances to create perspective expanding experiences. You can consciously create your own.' Be it in product development, business growth, expanding operations or projects, this value statement asks you to take the challenge head on.

In Life

Historically, feudal, religious and political systems have thrived by exploiting others' weaknesses rather than succeeding on their own strengths. Instead of creating infrastructure, systems and opportunities for weaker sections of society to become strong, we perpetuate their weaknesses and limitations so that they continue to be marginalized and forever under our control. Unscrupulous capitation fees, huge interest on money-lending to have-nots, fraudulent overseas job agents, exorbitant hospital fees, earnings through expired drugs...all these represent exploitation of the unaware and gullible masses—*asanthaa adikarathu*.

Asaraama adikarathu—being aware and vigilant—calls for leading life with foresight and focus. This would include planning your future, providing for rainy days, avoiding procrastination. Protect your risks with insurance and safeguards, discharge your duties before others remind you, don't be indifferent and lazy but be wide awake to the opportunities of life—and never exploit those who are weaker than you.

Message
Be proactive and don't exploit the weaknesses of others for personal gain

~Value Statement~

19

Film: *Annamalai*

*'Kettuponavan vazhalam aana nallaa
vazhnthavan kettu poga koodathu'*

'Wrongdoers may exist,
but the good should
not turn to evil'

In Business

On the face of it, this may appear to be a merely philosophical statement. In reality, this is a warning, a note of caution. History has shown that there are only a few organizations that have not only withstood tough times, uncertainties, economic meltdowns, political instability, riots and even threat on account of global terrorism, but have also consolidated their operations and grown.

Sometimes, organizations that were written off have challenged analysts and market-watchers by coming out of the red with far better innovation, better strategies, better teams, better management and increased productivity. These organizations which were once dismissed bounced back to glory sooner or later due to the efforts of great teams or visionaries who saw value in the organizations and helped them rebuild their lost glory. Satyam is a case in point: a company that was completely written off because of a muti-crore accounting fraud returned to existence due to the confidence of the human resources who believed in themselves. The entire work force of Satyam is trying to bring back the glory that was lost primarily because of the misdeeds of one person or a small group of people. However, this would not have been possible had the entire organization turned to practising unethical methods.

A prudent organization will have many checks and balances to ensure that it is ready to face any challenge and retain its reputation forever. Today, we see many reputed groups, including Tata and Infosys, strategize their succession plans much in advance. Such plans safeguard the interests of the organization, and ensure that the glory built doesn't suffer due to improper or inadequate planning. Consequently, despite potential misconduct on the part of individuals, these organizations can thrive on the foundation of hard work and avoidance of wrongdoing.

In Life

This value statement clearly indicates the importance of caution. Each one of us must have seen or heard about families that lived gloriously but suddenly lost everything and are now in immense pain and sorrow. It is not easy for a family that has lived for generations with great reputation and pride to hold on to its glory over the course of time. It is particularly the duty of the younger generation to maintain and further grow the reputation built painstakingly, brick by brick, by the earlier generation. This calls for discipline, focus, caution and foresight.

One needs to watch every action and deed and ensure that one doesn't fall into any trap of unlawful or evil activities. As Ralph Waldo Emerson states, 'It requires a great deal of boldness and a great deal of caution to make a good fortune, and when you have it, it requires ten times as much skill to keep it.' This growth and maintenance of one's fortunes can only be accomplished through hard work and good practices, even if one sees others getting ahead in the short term through unethical conduct.

Message
Caution, caution and caution—nothing is more vital to ensure that we don't fall from glory

~*Value Statement*~

20

Film: *Basha*

*'Namma vaazhkai namma
kailathaan irruku'*

✱

'Our life is in our hands'

In Business

According to Jack Welch, the business legend, 'Control your destiny or someone else will.' He goes on to say that good businesses create their vision, articulate the vision, passionately own the vision and relentlessly drive it to completion. A successful organization does not wait for external factors to grow and develop; it creates prospects so that it can get ahead and achieve its potential. It is indeed true, as William Jennings Bryan said, that 'Destiny is not a matter of chance, it is a matter of choice; it is not a thing to be waited for, it is a thing to be achieved.' A good organization will take charge of a situation and carve out opportunities even though they seem non-existent. .

In Life

Aham brahmasmi, the core of Indian philosophy, perhaps answers the apparently simple question: *namma vazhkai namma kailathaan irruku*—who determines the destiny of every human being? For the religious person, the answer is God; for the aetheist, it is the rational mind; for many others, the answer is unfathomable. The simple truth is that we—each one of us—create our own world and determine our own destiny through our own actions. The statement *aham brahmasmi* can thus be interpreted as 'I am the creator of my life'.

What does this mean for day-to-day living? In our journey of life, each one of us is constantly encountering options; through acts of omission and commission, we make our choices. The experiences of our life and what unfolds in the future are integrated outcomes of these choices. The wise man truly realizes this, and is therefore fully aware and takes complete responsibility for his actions. Those who do not engage in conscious living meander through life, get pushed around by other people's diktats and impositions, are enslaved by 'compulsions' and feel miserable and all the time. The result is that they continuously blame everything other except themselves and completely abdicate their responsibility of taking charge of their own lives.

At an individual level, this value statement calls for a mature mind to have complete ownership of one's life and to understand that, even though none of the external circumstances of life are within our control, each and every response to such situations are completely within our control. Life is what we make of it.

Message
Determine your own destiny

Film: *Arunachalam*

'Sollraan...senjittaan'

✷

'I committed...I delivered'

In Business

The strongest grouse against leaders—be it social, political or in the corporate world—is that though they make grand visionary statements about change, their actions fail to match their words. If leaders and managers want to implement change, accept newer ways of doing business and create the organization they desire, the first maxim to follow is embodied in this value statement: walk the talk.

As Mahatma Gandhi had said, 'Be the change you wish to see in this world'—and it will happen. There is nothing more encouraging for employees than observing their bosses perform what they expect from others. When a policy or procedural change is made by a manager, he or she too must follow it to the letter; one cannot expect employees to comply if the rule-makers do not.

If the leader himself or herself implements a change, becomes part of the team, acts and contributes instead of merely directing, then such leadership earns greater trust and respect from followers. To implement change, a leader has to literally take the lead—roll up your sleeve, get your hands dirty, wipe your brow and say, 'I did not just say it but I also did it'— *sollraan, senjittaan*. It is for this reason that the sports goods company Nike has found such appreciation for its tagline: 'Just do it'.

In Life

According to the Chinese philosopher Confucius, 'The superior man is modest in his speech but excels in his actions.' When you commit to something but don't work towards fulfilling your commitment, you end up feeling overwhelmed and powerless. However, when you act on it, you experience a sense of accomplishment which comes from knowing that you are getting better, that you are becoming a person of integrity.

In everyday life, you must take time to deliberate; but when it is time for action, stop thinking and get on with performing the required deeds. Whether you are a parent or a child, a sibling or a friend, a student or a teacher, a politician or a social worker, an activist or a volunteer, it is just not enough to make promises. You will become a valued person only when you keep your word: you must be not merely *sollraan* but also *senjittaan* or deliverer—a man of integrity.

Message
Live the promise, walk the talk

~Value Statement~

22

Film: *Muthu*

*'Naanga kodutha vakkum kodutha
porulaiyum thiruppi vangarathae illai'*

✱

'We don't take back the word
or the things we give'

In Business

This is yet another statement that emphasizes the power of integrity and commitment. In today's corporate world, long-term orientation and principled behaviour often seem to be taking a backseat while short-term opportunism and convenience appear to dominate decision-making and actions.

We have all too often seen organizations going back on commitments made to its stakeholders, especially employees. When faced with a small challenge in the market or economic environment, the first step most management bodies take is to go back on commitments related to employee compensation.

On the one hand, organizations give employees the semblance of security and stability; yet, at the slightest pretext, they do not hesitate to go back on commitments for project completion, compensation and payments, not to mention customer service. This is not to say that one must never reverse any decision—there is merit in careful discretion in situations where compensation, etc., may be contingent on performance; this statement only calls for farsightedness while making commitments and deploying the maximum possible resources to fulfil them.

In a philosophical sense, this value statement also upholds the truth of life being a cyclical process—if you operate with an 'investment approach', you would probably not in the long run regret the decisions made.

In Life

At a personal level, this is all about building trust. It also supports the dharmic tenet of benevolence—that one should always have the large-heartedness to give unconditionally, without expectation of any returns...and the law of karma would automatically reward one in its own way. If one makes a commitment and upholds it, the commitments made to one will also be honoured. When it comes to material things, never go back on what was promised and never take away anything that has already been given. Merely practise the lesson taught by Value Statement 5, and this too will automatically fall in place.

Message
Don't go back on your promises

~Value Statement~

Film: *Padaiyappa*

'Kashtapadaama ethuvum kidaikathu,
kashtapadama kidaikarathu
ennaikume nilaikathu'

✦

'You don't get something without real effort; even if you get it without effort, it won't stay with you for long'

In Business

Good luck cannot replace hard work in any endeavour. According to Stephen Leacock, 'I am a great believer in luck, and I find the harder I work the more I find of it.' For instance, Sachin Tendulkar overcame Shane Warne's leg spin not by luck but through sheer hard work.

This value statement teaches us that we need to work hard to be lucky. *Fortes fortuna adiuvat*—fortune favours the brave. No businessman, entrepreneur or CEO has reached his or her pedestal through plain luck. All of them have worked hard to rise up the ladder, and their efforts have paid off. No matter the accusations made against them out of spite or jealousy, it is not luck but hard work that has helped them to succeed. In essence, there is no shortcut to success—the only formula is hard work.

It sometimes appears to the onlooker that an organization is enjoying tremendous success without making any considerable effort; but it is observed that such an organization inevitably falls behind after a while and eventually crumbles. Good fortune that is coincidental—and not carved out for oneself by one's dedication and actions—is inevitably transient. Lasting success is founded on the bedrock of hard work.

In Life

Nothing comes easy in life. And what comes easy generally doesn't last. Chance probably plays an important part in our lives, but we cannot depend only on the 'luck factor'. We must understand and accept the truth of the proverb 'No pain, no gain'. It underlines the importance of assuming responsibilities in life, taking on challenges, performing under pressure, working hard to achieve success, and ultimately enjoying the fruits of it. This journey along this path of challenges, effort, uncertainty, perseverance, trials and tribulations makes the success waiting for us at the end of the road taste even sweeter.

On the other hand, if everything is handed to us on a platter, we take things for granted and start believing that we are lucky. Very soon, this tendency begins to breed complacence and creates the illusion that we are 'chosen ones' who automatically deserve the good things in life. It is important to realize that to deserve anything one needs to first serve, which can only be done by a combination of initiative and effort. Such an attitude to life reaps rich rewards—wealth, position, power, and more.

Message
Luck favours only those who work hard

Film: *Basha*

'Vaazhkaila bayam irrukalam, aana bayamae vazhkai ayuda koodathu'

★

'It is okay to fear some things in our life, but fear itself should not rule our life'

In Business

According to Confucius, 'The way of the superior man is threefold... Virtuous, he is free from anxieties; wise, he is free from perplexities; bold, he is free from fear.'

Fear is a virus; if allowed a breeding place in our minds, it will control our whole self, eat away at our spirit and block the path to success. Fear is the greatest enemy of progress and it should be conquered with courage. It requires courage to transform your dreams into reality, and only a few possess this quality. Ask any successful business enterprise—courage will have its due place of importance in the story of its evolution. The Hungarian author Kate Seredy says, 'Kill the snake of doubt in your soul, crush the worm of fear in your heart, and mountains will move out of your way.'

From the simplest policy implementation to a major IT application, from handling an irate customer to appraising an ineffective employee, from planning a major coup to putting into action a complex marketing strategy—everything requires courage. Without courage, a team or an organization will find it difficult to face uncertainties, failures, shortfalls and losses.

Most rags-to-riches stories—even in the corporate world— are products of the courage of visionaries. Without courage, the best of practices cannot shape a successful organization. Albert Einstein rightly said, 'Any intelligent fool can make things bigger and more complex... It takes a touch of genius and a lot of courage to move in the opposite direction.' Courage, thus, is the most important element when one is trying to make a mark for oneself in today's fiercely competitive world.

In Life

William Shakespeare wrote in Julius Caesar, 'Cowards die many times before their deaths. The valiant never taste of death but once.' Realistically speaking, not everyone has the automatic courage to stand up to others and confront challenges boldly. And one may be afraid of converting one's thoughts into action. One needs to fight and overcome fear—*vaazhkaila bayam irukkalam*—and learn to encounter dangers and difficulties with firmness. Fear is required to foresee challenges and courage is required to tackle them and move ahead. But if only the former exists, rest assured that life is going to be a disaster—*bayame vaazhkkai ayuda koodathu*.

Message
Fear should not rule us; rather, it should prepare us better

~*Value Statement*~

Film: *Baba*

'Baba counting starts now... 1, 2, 3...'

In Business

In his play *The Merry Wives of Windsor*, William Shakespeare wrote, '[B]etter three hours too soon than a minute too late'. Time is of the essence in all situations. This simple value statement calls attention to the importance of timelines—be it in devising a strategy, launching a product, hiring the right person or firing the wrong one, making a purchase or sale, executing a project, launching an IPO, and so on. In fact, in all facets of an organization, timelines are of utmost importance. An organization can never overcome a roadblock or mitigate a risk until it reviews its status on the planned timelines.

The great dividing line between the success and failure of an organization can be expressed thus: 'It did not have the time'. The finest hour for a manager is when he gets things done and the worst is when things are delayed. The countdown to completion highlighted in the value statement emphasizes the fact that procrastination is the most deadly disease in any organization and requires immediate cure. As the American tycoon Malcolm S. Forbes had said, 'One worthwhile task carried to a successful conclusion is worth half-a-hundred half-finished tasks.'

In Life

According to Charles Darwin, 'A man who dares to waste one hour of time has not discovered the value of life.' The value statement upholds this sentiment and reminds us that procrastination is an evil that we must at all times battle. We cannot afford to get into the habit of procrastinating, no matter what the reason. Setting personal deadlines and working towards them is the first step leading to the pathway of success. As Anthony Robbins says, 'Once you have mastered time, you will understand how true it is that most people overestimate what they can accomplish in a year—and underestimate what they can achieve in a decade!' The value statement also indicates that while ordinary people merely think of spending time the great think of using it.

Set timelines for all tasks—even your day-to-day activities and chores—and review the progress; you will be surprised to see how much efficiency this brings into your life and how much time you will have for other things.

Message
Time is the most precious thing—do not waste it

Film: *Sivaji*

***

'Saavara naal therunjipochuna
vazhara naal naragam aayudum'

✴

'If you know when you will die, your life will be hell'

In Business

Businesses are established to succeed and flourish—not to fold up and die. There is no guarantee of success in business, but a pessimistic view about its future will certainly lead to its eventual death. The same holds good for any new project, product or service.

Here, it is important to know the difference between pessimism and assessing risks. Business risk assessment is a way of determining what can go wrong and what action is required to mitigate such situations, while pessimism is merely figuring out what will go wrong and doing nothing about it.

Organizations cultivate optimism by committing to a cause, a plan or a value system. Only with these guidelines will they grow in a desired direction and be able to rise above day-to-day challenges and occasional setbacks.

According to Winston Churchill, 'An optimist sees an opportunity in every calamity; a pessimist sees a calamity in every opportunity.' A positive attitude is contagious—and every manager needs to possess this quality for his or her team to perform well.

In Life

Hope is the biggest motivator in life. It is the thin line between certainty and doubt. It is a kind of no man's land, where no guarantees are available in spite of all the competence and talents an individual may possess—and yet, one must persevere. The very absence of guarantees is what leads to imaginative thinking, efforts and pursuit.

Imagine if life was predictable and the future was guaranteed... We have ample lessons to learn from the lives of people who are born with a silver spoon in their mouths. In most such cases, the second generation, which has had a comfortable life, with nothing to fear, turns out to be non-enterprising, arrogant and lazy—whittling away the hard-earned wealth of the first generation. In a larger sense, it is as if they know what is fated for them (their 'moment of death') and become complacent—and this complacence leads to their destruction. On the other hand, there are seemingly ordinary people whose only possessions in life may be hopes and dreams. They are frequently confronted by misery and challenges, and every day may pose yet another question mark about the future. Even then, such people bravely face the odds, are determined to redefine their lives and make the impossible possible with single-minded dedication and a fierce desire to make it big, Such is the life story of achievers, whether in the field of business, commerce, science, arts or cinema. None of these people have any guarantees in life— and yet, with optimism, determination and perseverance, they manage to succeed against all odds.

Message
Life is interesting because it is unpredictable; be positive

Film: *Muthu*

*'Kedaikiradhu kedaikkaama
irukkaadhu. Kedaikaama
irukaradhu kedaikkaathu'*

★

'What you are entitled to, you will certainly get; what is not for you, you will not get'

In Business

This statement reflects a very interesting philosophy, almost challenging one of the premises of most corporate endeavours—'get it at any cost'.

What are the consequences of this 'get it anyhow' attitude? It gives licence for deceitful actions, underhanded tricks and unprincipled aggression to gain an advantage—and this often abets people to adopt any method as long as they achieve their objective. We are entitled to making attempts to achieve our goals, but they must be honest, whole-hearted and principled attempts. What we are destined to, we will get. So says the karma principle.

Unprincipled actions and practices, often legitimized by reason of ambitious targets for growth and a concern for numbers alone, only act as short-term drugs which create an illusion of success. Ultimately, one will get what one deserves. The long-term growth, success and achievements of an organization depend on the efforts, methods and processes deployed by it.

The important management lesson given by this value statement is to stay focused on the objective, and then the management must make all efforts to attain the objective in an ethical manner. The most significant factor that should drive the management is hope. Many a time, we may feel that we can completely control the effort but not the outcome; but even if the results fall short of expectations, the management should not lose hope. Another secondary management lesson to be drawn from this powerful statement is that we need to move away from unrealistic numbers and have realistic goals that we can achieve, and thus deserve.

In Life

In Indian philosophy, this is the dharmic way: giving due credence to destiny—the cyclical flow of life—wherein everything balances out appropriately. Yet, there must be no lack of serious effort by the individual in working towards his goals. We should pursue our goals with dedication, like a good sportsman playing a game, but recognize that the outcome is not necessarily a controllable factor. Such detached yet serious pursuit can also be described as *nishkama karma*—selfless action performed without any expectation of results.

A popular Indian proverb also encapsulates the message of this value statement: *daane daane pe likha hai khaane wale ka naam*—every grain has inscribed upon it the name of the person who is destined to consume it. We will receive what is fated for us—and what we deserve will come to us. The mature mind possesses this quality of acceptance of outcomes regardless of the efforts put in. If we can embrace this principle, there will be no sense of demotivation, deprivation, loss of interest or loss of faith in oneself—even if the results fail to meet expectations.

Message
Effort is more important than the outcome

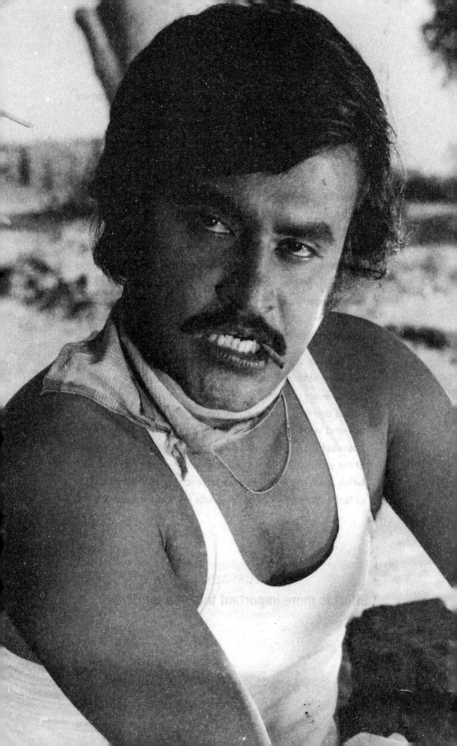

28

Film: *16 Vayathinile*

'Ithu eppadi irukku'

✦

'How is this?'

In Business

When it comes to teamwork, silence is not golden—it is deadly. Getting the opinion of team members is very important for any manager. No matter how organizations are structured—whether there are specialized departments or strategic business units—it is the teams within those structures that spell success. If the manager wants to ensure that the team is coming together, keeping together and working together, the members must be given the chance to express their opinions and also showcase their efforts. *Ithu eppadi irukku* exemplifies this phenomenon—it is important to ask others 'How is this?'

While it is the role of the manager or team leader to obtain opinions from his team members, the members too have a responsibility to express their opinions and share their knowledge. When teams outgrow their individual performances and members share their knowledge and efforts and speak up, excellence becomes a habit. Albert Einstein highlighted this clearly when he said, 'Great spirits have always encountered violent opposition from mediocre minds. The mediocre mind is incapable of understanding the man who refuses to bow blindly to conventional prejudices and chooses instead to express his opinions courageously and honestly.' We must strive to rise above the mediocre and solicit others' opinions on any matter, as well as volunteer our own.

In Life

We can apply this statement to all walks of life—situations involving friends, family, political parties and even the whole country—and realize what is being missed. Opinions are taken for granted, perspectives are changed by browbeating others, and sometimes even a whimper of an idea is quickly mutilated. The effective functioning of any team or social unit depends on how the opinion of its members is invited, considered, how conversations are facilitated and how decisions are accepted and implemented by the unit. The art of building and maintaining a happy and harmonious family also revolves around the same principles: listen to others' points of view and do not take anything or anybody for granted.

Message
Opinion matters

~*Value Statement*~

Film: *Basha*

*'Naama nammala gavanichhaathan
aandavan nammala gavanipaan'*

★

'Only when we take
care of ourselves will
God take care of us'

In Business

Business wisdom comprises the possession of wide experience and knowledge together with the ability to apply the same consistently and appropriately. Every entrepreneur, business organization and professional goes through the following stages while acquiring business wisdom: the novice, the advanced beginner, the competent, the proficient and the master. None of these stages is the outcome of prayers, fortune or good luck—it is progress obtained through sheer hard work. However, this doesn't mean prayers are not necessary; they are, but only when any task has been given the best shot. Praying without making an effort is useless.

Self-discipline, professional integrity and ethical conduct are difficult to sustain in business life, but hard work is the key to achieving high standards. Prayers are surely going to help you—provided you do your best. That is the essence of this value statement.

In Life

The old Vedic saying 'work is worship' exhorts us to do our job honestly—work is akin to praying to God. And the Bhagavad Gita says, 'Do your duty without expectations.' Commitment, duty and self-discipline are the values that most scriptures emphasize. When we think that prayers alone will solve our problems, we prove ourselves weak as human beings, looking to escape our responsibilities and hoping that God will save us. God will only answer the prayers of those who are self-disciplined, hard-working, self-sufficient and content, for He knows that they have done their job well and it is His turn to support them.

There is another interesting message in this statement. For those of us who believe that God may be found in anyone, it is even more important to take care of ourselves—the God within—and God will ultimately bless us. Take care of your habits, ethics, personality and overall wellness, and God will be happy to bless you with even more. As Edward Bouverie Pusey had said, 'Practise in life whatever you pray for, and God will give it you more abundantly.'

Message
God helps those who help themselves

Music Launch of *Chandramukhi*

'Naan yaanai illa, kuthirai, keezha vizhundha takkunu yezhunthupaen'

★

'I am not an elephant but a horse, for I get up instantly when I fall'

In Business

This value statement refers to the elephant which finds it difficult to quickly get back on its feet when it falls—the same can be said of organizations. Being a giant can often create an illusion of strength. Sheer size may carry with it its own burdens and limitations. Although the larger-than-life aspect of a business behemoth can be awe-inspiring and intimidating, the same thing could also make it slow or sometimes even immobilize it—when there is a setback, the organization finds it hard to recoup and move forward again.

On the other hand, truly great organizations are dynamic and energetic rather than simply being large. They must possess agility, which would help them to be as swift as their competitors—sometimes even better. The agility and flexibility of an organization helps it make quick changes and adapt to new challenges as they emerge. It is that quality which would help it to bounce back and be on its feet even after an almost disastrous fall. Agility is the core competence of the 'horse' in this statement.

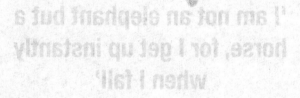

'I am not an elephant but a horse, for I get up instantly when I fall'

In Life

We all need to be agile not only in business but in our personal lives as well. More than physical agility, it is agility of the mind that matters. A person with a quick mind possesses self-confidence. Circumstances do not bring things to a halt for him or her; they do not even make such a person pause. If there is a step back, it is conscious and strategic. If there is an unexpected blow, the determination to bounce back is multiplied. 'Never say die' is their spirit.

The value statement re-emphasizes the need to look at failure as the next opportunity. As Henry Wadsworth Longfellow said, 'Look not mournfully into the past, it comes not back again. Wisely improve the present, it is thine. Go forth to meet the shadowy future without fear and with a manly heart.' Move on, re-energize yourself and gallop to success.

Note: The punchline used here is not from any Rajinikanth film but from a very powerful statement he made at the release of the music album of his film Chandramukhi. *His previous film* Baba *failed at the box office—and failure of a film of this superstar is considered unacceptable by his fans and the industry. During the launch of* Chandramukhi, *this remarkable man said, with a clap of his hands,* 'Naan yaanai illa, kuthirai, keezha vizhundha takkunnu yezhunthupaen.' Chandramukhi *went on to create box office history.*

Message
When you fall, get up...and get up quickly

Acknowledgements

No venture big or small is completed without the help of a few good people who are always willing to extend their support and assistance when sought. I wholeheartedly thank the following people who helped me complete this book. All of them gave me their support, with a lot of happiness and a smile on their lips.

Raja Krishnamoorthy, who was highly instrumental in making this book comprehensive and interesting;

My good friend Avis, who was the first person with whom I shared the idea of the book and got the encouragement to go ahead;

My wife Sunita and my children Arjun and Jayanth, for their encouragement and for sacrificing many weekends to my preoccupation with this book;

Ramky (Ram N. Ramakrishnan), for his great help with the content;

Meena Rajakrishnamoorthy, for suggesting a fabulous title for this book;

Still photographer Gnanam, Film News Anandan and Sundar of onlysuperstar.com, for helping me with the relevant photographs;

The dialogue writers and directors of the films in which these punchlines were delivered by Rajinikanth;

My closest friends, especially Srini and Sankar, for their encouragement.

My thanks to New Horizon Media—especially to Badri Sheshadri, for readily agreeing to publish this first book of mine; and to Vaidehi Sankaran, for putting up with me till the book was published. My special thanks to Rupa Publications India, for taking this book to a national and international audience—to Kapish Mehra in particular, for facilitating the publication of this edition; and to Pradipta Sarkar, with whom I have thoroughly enjoyed working. It has been a fascinating journey all through.

P.C. Balasubramanian

Praise for the Book

'[V]ery innovative, crisp and exciting. [*Rajini's Punchtantra*] can also have an international readership.'
—Ravi Subramanian, President and CEO, Shriram City Union Finance,
and author of *If God Was a Banker* and *The Incredible Banker*

'[W]hile you've probably enjoyed Rajini's dialogues in the movies and remember them all, you may not have figured the deeper significance of those lines—and the messages they hold for us in business and in life. [This book] takes you on a fascinating journey reliving those dialogues, connecting the dots and revealing invaluable life lessons. It's the kind of book you will want to go back to—again and again... A must read!'
—Prakash Iyer, MD, Kimberly Clark, and author of
The Habit of Winning

'[T]his ageing hero's filmy punchlines have always ignited resounding applause in cinema halls... [A] book like [*Rajini's Punchtantra*] was perhaps waiting to happen.'

—*Deccan Herald*

'[This book] is entertaining on the surface but is layered with meaning... [It] serves as ammunition for your next big meeting: quote a Rajini punchline and relate it to the way you work or live your life!'

—*Ritz*

'The book is a must-read for everyone. There is a lesson to be learnt in every punchline—and if you...missed it when Rajini said it, Bala and Raja make sure you don't. Mind it.'

—*Galatta*

'The superstar ruled yesterday, rules today and will continue to rule. So much to learn from him, and this book is just the beginning...'

—*Inbox 1305*

'[*Rajini's Punchtantra*] links a select thirty punchlines of the superstar to business mantras that could be the bible for every corporate czar.'

—T.S. Sudhir, journalist

'I would have never read a book with a cine actor's face on the cover; but [this book] made the difference... My favourite: emphasis on brand equity through "*Paera kaetavudane chumma athuruthilae*"...'

—T.R. Santhanakrishnan, Chairman and CEO, TaurusQuest

'[The authors] have woven together management and life principles in a very concise manner...'

—Geetha Sellamuthu, Director, Sanghamitra Centre for Wellbeing

'[V]ery interesting, enjoyable and educative...'

—V. Subramanian, Cochin

'[We] can now use Rajini's movies and [this] book to teach our children, our future, simple but valuable life lessons...'

—Preeti Vinayak Shah, USA